MW00603303

by Knit Picks

Copyright 2017 © Knit Picks

All rights reserved. This book or any portion thereof may not be reproduced or used in any manner whatsoever without the express written permission of the publisher except for the use of brief quotations in a book review.

Photography by Amy Cave

Printed in the United States of America

First Printing, 2017

ISBN 978-1-62767-154-5

Versa Press, Inc
800-447-7829

www.versapress.com

CONTENTS

COMPASS CARDIGAN

by Kathryn Folkerth

FINISHED MEASUREMENTS

33 (36, 40.5, 43.5, 46.5, 48.5, 52)" finished bust measurement; garment is meant to be worn with 2" of ease

YARN

Knit Picks Stroll Sock Yarn (75% Superwash Merino Wool, 25% Nylon; 231 yards/50g): Dandelion 25024, 7 (8, 8, 9, 9, 10, 10) skeins

NEEDLES

US 3 (3.25mm) DPNs, or 1 size smaller than needle to obtain gauge

US 4 (3.5mm) 32" circular needles plus DPNs or two 24" circular needles for two circulars technique, or one 32" or longer circular needle for Magic Loop technique, or size to obtain gauge

NOTIONS

Yarn Needle
4 Stitch Markers
Scrap Yarn or Stitch Holder

GAUGE

26 sts and 32 rows = 4" in St st on larger needles, blocked

27 sts and 28 rows = 4" wide x 5" high over Chart A or E on larger needles, blocked

27 sts and 37 rows = 4" wide and 3.75" high over Chart B, C, or D on larger needles, blocked

Compass Cardigan

Notes:

This cardigan is worked flat in one piece to the underarms when live sts are put on hold for both fronts to be worked later. Centered lace panels run from hem to neck and side to side and intersect at the center back. The lace panels sections are individually charted. Charts B, C, and E are worked in succession over the same rows and the markers between them will have to be moved when the yarn overs and accompanying decreases run from one chart into the next. When working charts read RS rows (odd numbers) from right to left, and WS rows (even numbers) from left to right.

Seed Stitch (worked flat over an even number of sts)

Row 1 (RS): *K1, P1; rep from * to end of row.
Row 2 (WS): *P1, K1; rep from * to end of row.
Rep Rows 1-2 for pattern. If working over an odd number of sts, end RS rows as K1, begin WS rows as K1.

Stockinette Stitch (St st, worked flat or in the rnd over any number of sts)

Row 1 (RS): K.
Row 2 (WS): P.
Rep Rows 1-2 for pattern. To work in the rnd, K all rnds.

I-cord Bind Off

CO 3 sts onto the left needle. *K2, Sl1, K1, PSSO. Place 3 sts just worked back onto left needle. Repeat from * until all sts have been bound off.

DIRECTIONS

Body

The body is worked flat. Using circular needle CO 243 (263, 283, 303, 323, 343, 363) sts.

Row 1 (WS): P105 (115, 125, 135, 145, 155, 165) sts, PM, work next 3 sts in Seed st, PM, P27 sts, PM, work next 3 sts in Seed st, PM, P105 (115, 125, 135, 145, 155, 165) sts to end.
Row 2 (RS): K to first marker, SM, work in Seed St to next marker, SM, work Row 2 of Chart A to next marker, SM, work Seed st to last marker, SM, K to end.

Cont working as established through Row 23 of Chart A. Then work Rows 10-23 of Chart A 5 more times.

On the next row (RS), beginning with a purl st work Seed st to first marker, remove marker and cont in Seed st to second marker, SM, work Row 24 of Chart A to third marker, work in Seed st to end, removing last marker as you come to it. Cont as established for 2 more rows through the last row of Chart A.

Next Row (WS): Work Row 1 of Chart D to first marker, work Row 1 of Chart C to second marker, work Row 1 of Chart B to end. On the following row, work Row 2 of Chart B to first marker, work Row 2 of Chart C to second marker, work Row 2 of Chart D to end. Cont working as established through the completion of these three charts.

Next 3 Rows: Work in Seed st to first marker, SM, work Chart E to second marker, SM, work in Seed st to end.

On the following (WS) row, work in St st to 3 sts before first marker, PM, work next 3 sts in Seed st, SM, work Chart E to next marker, SM, work Seed st over next 3 sts, PM, work St st to end. Cont as established for another 24 (24, 20, 18, 16, 16, 12) rows.

On the next (RS) row, K first 67 (73, 76, 81, 86, 93, 97) sts and place them on holder for right front. Work next 109 (117, 131, 141, 151, 157, 169) Back sts in pattern. Place last 67 (73, 76, 81, 86, 93, 97) unworked sts on holder for left front.

Turn work and cont until the repeat of Chart E has been completed a total of 6 times then work Rows 15-25 of Chart E.

Row 26 (WS): P30 (31, 37, 41, 45, 47, 53) sts, BO next 49 (55, 57, 59, 61, 63, 63) sts, P to end and place all live sts on holders. Break yarn making sure to leave generous 3x length of a tail to later graft the shoulder sts together.

Pick up sts being held for right front and place them on needle. Beginning on the WS, work 66 (66, 70, 72, 74, 74, 78) rows.

Next Row: P30 (31, 37, 41, 45, 47, 53) sts, BO to end. Place 30 (31, 37, 41, 45, 47, 53) live sts on holder.

Pick up sts being held for left front and place them on needle. Beginning on the RS, work 67 (67, 71, 73, 75, 75, 79) rows.

Next Row: BO 37 (36, 34, 32, 30, 28, 45) sts, P remaining 30 (31, 37, 41, 45, 47, 53) sts and place them on holder.

Block piece to size.
Return sts being held for front and back of right shoulder to needles. With RSs facing each other, join sts via the 3 Needle Bind Off. Rep for other shoulder.

Attach an I-cord edge around the neck, side, and bottom edges of the sweater. Using smaller size DPNs, CO 4 sts. *K3, Sl1, PU a st from the selvedge edge and PSSO. Push sts to other end of the DPN and without turning work repeat from * until you have added an applied I-cord around the outer edges of the sweater.

Sleeves (make 2 the same)

PU 110 (110, 117, 120, 123, 123, 130) sts evenly around the armhole edge. K 1 rnd, PM and join in rnd.

Dec Rnd: K1, K2tog, K to last 3 sts, SSK, K1, SM. 2 sts dec.

Repeat Dec Rnd every 6th (6th, 5th, 5th, 5th, 6th, 5th) rnd 19 (19, 22, 22, 23, 23, 25) more times. 70 (70, 71, 74, 75, 75, 78) sts remain. Knit until sleeve measures 17 (17, 17, 17.5, 17.5, 18, 18)" from underarm.

BO using I-cord BO.

Finishing

Weave in ends, wash and block to size.

Chart A

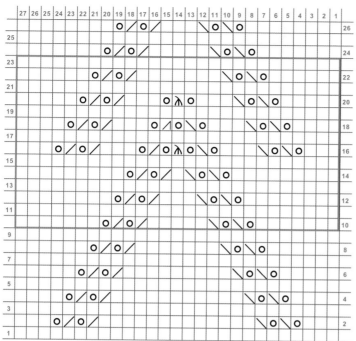

Legend

knit
RS: knit stitch
WS: purl stitch

yo
yarn over

ssk
RS: Slip one stitch as if to knit, Slip another stitch as if to knit. Insert left-hand needle into front of these 2 stitches and knit them together
WS: Purl two stitches together in back loops, inserting needle from the left, behind and into the backs of the 2nd & 1st stitches in that order

k2tog
RS: Knit two stitches together as one stitch
WS: Purl 2 stitches together

sl1 k2tog psso
slip 1, knit 2 tog, pass slipped stitch over k2tog

k3tog
RS: Knit three stitches together as one
WS: Purl three stitches together as one

knit tbl
RS: Knit stitch through back loop
WS: Purl stitch through back loop

pattern repeat

Chart B

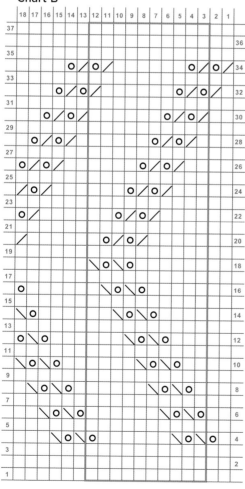

Chart C

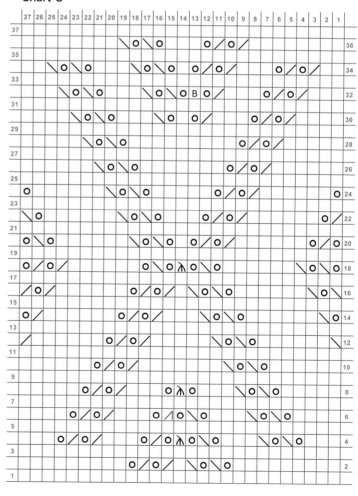

Chart D

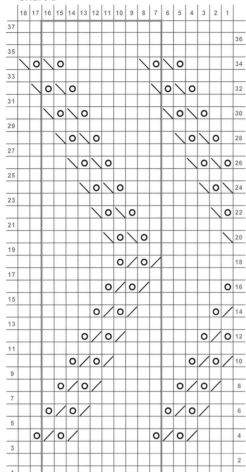

Chart E

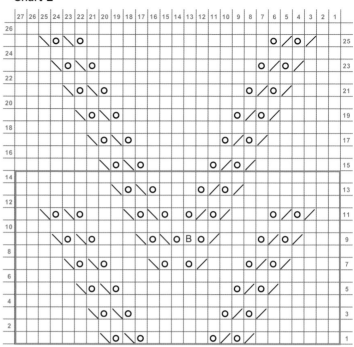

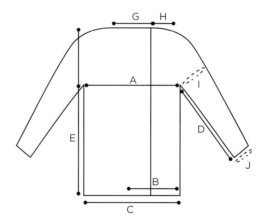

A 16.5 (18, 20.25, 21.75, 23.25, 24.25, 26)"
B 10.5 (11.25, 11.75, 12.5, 13.25, 14.25, 15)"
C 37.25 (40.25, 43.5, 46.5, 49.5, 52.5, 55.75)"
D 17 (17, 17, 17.5)[17.5, 18, 18)"
E 21.25 (21.25, 20.5, 20.25, 19.75, 19.75, 19)"
F 8.5 (8.5, 9, 9.25, 9.5, 9.5, 10)"
G 7.5 (8.5, 8.75, 9, 9.25, 9.5, 9.5)"
H 4.5 (4.75, 5.75, 6.25, 7, 7.25, 8.25"
I 17 (17, 18, 18.5, 19, 19, 20)"
J 10.75 (10.75, 11, 11.5, 11.5, 11.5, 12)"

COVELL TEE

by Tian Connaughton

FINISHED MEASUREMENTS

30 (34, 38, 42, 46, 50, 54, 58, 62)"
finished bust measurement; garment is
meant to be worn with 2" of positive ease

YARN

Knit Picks CotLin (70% Tanguis Cotton,
30% Linen; 123 yards/50g): Moroccan
Red 23996, 6 (7, 8, 9, 10, 11, 12, 13, 14) balls

NEEDLES

US 7 (4.5mm) straight or circular needles,
or size to obtain gauge
US 6 (4mm) DPNs or two 24" circular
needles for two circulars technique,
or one 32" or longer circular needle
for Magic Loop technique, or one size
smaller than needle used to obtain gauge

NOTIONS

Yarn Needle
Stitch Markers
Scrap Yarn or Stitch Holder

GAUGE

18 sts and 24 rows = 4" in St st on larger
needles, blocked

Covell Tee

Notes:
Covell is worked in pieces from the bottom up with shaping for the sleeves. Once the pieces are seamed, stitches are picked up on the sleeves to work the the ribbed cuff in the round.

K1, P1 Ribbing (worked in the rnd over an even number of sts)
Rnd 1: *K1, P1; rep from * around.
Rep Rnd 1 for pattern.

K2, P2 Ribbing (worked in the rnd over multiples of 4 sts)
Rnd 1: *K2, P2; rep from * around.
Rep Rnd 1 for pattern.

DIRECTIONS

Back
The back is worked flat from the bottom up.

Hem
With larger needles, CO 68 (76, 86, 94, 104, 112, 122, 130, 140) sts.

Rows 1-3: Knit.
Row 4 (WS): P1, *P2tog, YO; rep from * to last st, P1.
Rows 5-7: Knit.
Row 8: Purl.

Rep Rows 1-8 twice more.

Body
Work in St st until piece measure 14" from CO edge, ending with a WS row.

Shape Sleeves
Cont in St st, PM for beginning of sleeves, and using the cable cast-on method, CO 12 sts at beginning of next 4 rows.

CO 8 sts at beginning of next 2 rows.

CO 6 sts at beginning of next 2 rows.

CO 4 sts at beginning of next 2 rows. (42 total sts CO for each sleeve.) 152 (160, 170, 178, 188, 196, 206, 214, 224) sts.

Work until sleeves measure 6.25 (6.5, 6.75, 7, 7.25, 7.5, 7.75, 8, 8.25)", measuring at the sleeve cuff, ending with WS row.

Shape Shoulders and Sleeves
BO 4 sts at beginning of next 2 rows. 144 (152, 162, 170, 180, 188, 198, 206, 216) sts.

Next Row (RS): BO 4 sts, K to first sleeve marker, K16 (19, 23, 26, 29, 32, 36, 39, 43) sts, place next 36 (38, 40, 42, 46, 48, 50, 52, 54) sts for center back on holder, join new ball of yarn, K across to end of row.
Next Row (WS): BO 4 sts, P across row, using original ball of yarn after the held sts.

Work even until shoulders measure 8.25 (8.5, 8.75, 9, 9.25, 9.5, 9.75, 10, 10.25)", measuring at sleeve CO at marker.
BO shoulder and sleeve sts.

Front
Work front same as back, completing all CO for sleeve, working in St st until sleeves measure 5.25 (5.5, 5.75, 6, 6.25, 6.5, 6.75, 7, 7.25)", measuring at sleeve CO at marker, ending with a WS row.

Left Front
(RS): K across to first sleeve marker, K27 (30, 34, 37, 40, 43, 47, 50, 54) sts, turn.
(WS): BO 4 st, P to end of row.

Sizes 30 (34, 38)" only
BO 3 sts at beginning of next 2 WS rows.
BO 1 st at beginning of next WS row.

Sizes 42 (46, 50, 54, 58, 62)" only
BO 2 sts at beginning of next 3 WS rows.
BO 1 st at beginning of next WS row.

All Sizes
Work even in St st until sleeves measure 6.25 (6.5, 6.75, 7, 7.25, 7.5, 7.75, 8, 8.25)", measuring at the sleeve cuff, ending with WS row.

Shape Shoulders and Sleeves
BO 4 sts at beginning of next 2 RS rows.

Work even until shoulders measure 8.25 (8.5, 8.75, 9, 9.25, 9.5, 9.75, 10, 10.25)", measuring at sleeve CO at marker.

BO shoulder and sleeve sts.

Right Front
(RS): With RS facing, place center 14 (16, 18, 20, 24, 26, 28, 30, 32) sts on holder for front neck, join yarn, BO 4 sts at neck edge, K to end of row.

Sizes 30 (34, 38)" only
BO 3 sts at beginning of next 2 RS rows.
BO 1 st at beginning of next RS row.

Sizes 42 (46, 50, 54, 58, 62)" only
BO 2 sts at beginning of next 3 RS rows.
BO 1 st at beginning of next RS row.

All Sizes
Work even in St st until sleeve measures 6.25 (6.5, 6.75, 7, 7.25, 7.5, 7.75, 8, 8.25)", measuring at the sleeve cuff, ending with RS row.

Shape Shoulders and Sleeves
BO 4 sts at beginning of next 2 WS rows.
Work even until shoulders measure 8.25 (8.5, 8.75, 9, 9.25, 9.5, 9.75, 10, 10.25)", measuring at sleeve CO at marker.

BO shoulder and sleeve sts.

Finishing
Block each piece.
Using preferred method, seam across shoulder to sleeve cuff.
Leaving about 3" unworked at hem, seam up each side to sleeve cuff.

Neckline
Starting at left shoulder seam and with RS facing, pick up sts at a rate of 3 sts for every 4 rows and each st from holders, ending with an even number of sts, PM at beginning of rnd.

Work in K1, P1 Ribbing for 3 rnds.

BO all sts.

Sleeve Ribbing

With smaller needles and beginning at underarm seam, PU and K
40 (40, 44, 44, 48, 48, 52, 52, 56) sts evenly around cuff, join to
work in the rnd, PM to indicate beginning of round.
Work in K2, P2 Ribbing for 4".
BO loosely in pattern.

Weave in all remaining ends. Block entire piece again if needed.

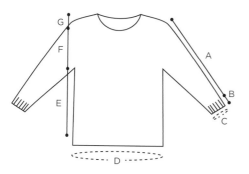

A 9.25"
B 4"
C 7.25 (7.25, 7.75, 8, 8.25, 8.5, 8.75, 9, 9.5)"
D 30 (34, 38, 42, 46, 50, 54, 58, 62)"
E 14"
F 8.25, 8.5, 8.75, 9, 9/25, 9.5, 9.75, 10, 10.25)"
G 3"

STRIPED SHRUG

by Hannah DeBoer

FINISHED MEASUREMENTS

34.75 (38.25, 42, 46.25, 50)" finished bust measurement; garment is meant to be worn with 2" of positive ease

YARN

Knit Picks Shine Sport (60% Pima Cotton, 40% Modal; 110 yards/50g): MC Cream 23615, 4 (4, 4, 5, 5) balls. C1 Grapefruit 25778, 3 (4, 4, 4, 5) balls

NEEDLES

US 4 (3.5mm) 32" circular needles, or size to obtain gauge

NOTIONS

Yarn Needle
Stitch Markers
Stitch Holder

GAUGE

24 sts and 32 rows = 4" in St st, blocked

Striped Shrug

Notes:

Garter St (worked flat)
All Rows: Knit.

Stockinette Stitch (St st, worked flat)
Row 1: Knit.
Row 2: Purl.
Rep Rows 1-2 for pattern.

DIRECTIONS

Body

Using MC, CO 208 (230, 252, 278, 300) sts. Do not join into the rnd.

Work in Garter St for 8 rows, slipping the first two sts of every row.

Switch to C1 and work 8 rows in St st beginning with a RS row, slipping the first two sts of every row.
Switch to MC and work 8 rows in St st, slipping the first two sts of every row.

Continue in this way, working 8 rows of each color in St st until piece measures about 12 (12, 12, 14, 14)". End with an 8 row stripe of C1.

Dividing Row (RS): Sl 2 sts WYIB, K 46 (50, 54, 58, 64) sts for right front, BO 12 (12, 14, 16, 18) sts, K 88 (102, 112, 126, 132) sts for back, BO 12 (12, 14, 16, 18) sts, K 48 (52, 56, 60, 66) sts to end for left front.

You will be working on the left front. Place the back and right front sts on stitch holders.

Left Front

Switch to MC.

Size 34.75" Only
Next Row (WS): Sl 2 sts WYIF, P to end.
Dec Row 1 (RS): K 2, SSK, K to end. 1 st dec.
Dec Row 2: Sl 2 sts WYIF, P to last 4 sts, P2tog TBL, P2. 1 st dec.
Rep the last two dec rows one more time. 44 sts.
Dec Row 3: K 2, SSK, K to end. 1 st dec.
Next Row: Sl 2 sts WYIF, P to end.

Rep Dec Row 3 1 more time. 42 sts.

Switch to C1.

Shape Neckline
Dec Row 1 (WS): Sl 2 WYIF, P to end
Dec Row 2 (RS): K to last 6 sts, K2tog, K 4. 1 st dec.
Dec Row 3: Sl 2 WYIF, P to end.
Dec Row 4: K to end.
Next Row: Sl 2 WYIF, P to end.

Rep Dec Rows 2-4 once more. 40 sts.
Switch to MC.

Rep Dec Rows 1-4 twice more. 38 sts.

*Switch to C1. Rep Dec Rows 1-4 twice more. Switch to MC.

Beginning with a WS row (and slipping the first 2 sts of every WS row), work in St st for 8 rows. Rep from * once more. 34 sts. Armhole should measure 6.5".

Switch to C1 and beginning with a WS row (and slipping the first 2 sts of every WS row), work 5 rows in St st.

Sizes 38.25" and 42" Only
Next Row (WS): Sl 2 sts WYIF, P to end.
Dec Row 1 (RS): K 2, SSK, K to end. 1 st dec.
Dec Row 2: Sl 2 sts WYIF, P to last 4 sts, P2tog TBL, P2. 1 st dec.

Rep the last two dec rows one more time. 48 (52) sts.

Dec Row 3: K 2, SSK, K to end. 1 st dec.
Next Row : Sl 2 sts WYIF, P to end.

Rep Dec Row 3 1 more time. 46 (50) sts.
Switch to C1.

Shape Neckline
Dec Row 1 (WS): Sl 2 WYIF, P to end
Dec Row 2 (RS): K to last 6 sts, K2tog, K 4. 1 st dec.
Dec Row 3: Sl 2 WYIF, P to end.
Dec Row 4: K to end.
Next Row: Sl 2 WYIF, P to end.
Rep Dec Rows 2-4 once more. 44 (48) sts.

Switch to MC.

Rep Dec Rows 1-4 twice more. 42 (46) sts.

*Switch to C1. Rep Dec Rows 1-4 twice more. Switch to MC. Beginning with a WS row (and slipping the first 2 sts of every WS row), work in St st for 8 rows. Rep from * once more. 38 (42) sts.

Then switch to C1 and beginning with a WS row (and slipping the first 2 sts of every WS row), work 8 rows in St st.

Armhole should measure 8".

Switch to MC and beginning with a WS row (and slipping the first 2 sts of every WS row), work 5 rows in St st.

Sizes 46.25" and 50" Only
Next Row (WS): Sl 2 sts WYIF, P to end.
Dec Row 1 (RS): K 2, SSK, K to end. 1 st dec.
Dec Row 2: Sl 2 sts WYIF, P to last 4 sts, P2tog TBL, P2. 1 st dec.

Rep the last two dec rows one more time. 56 (62) sts.

Dec Row 3: K 2, SSK, K to end. 1 st dec.
Next Row: Sl 2 sts WYIF, P to end.

Rep dec row 3 1 more time. 54 (60) sts.
Switch to C1.

Shape Neckline
Dec Row 1: Sl 2 WYIF, P to end
Dec Row 2: K to last 6 sts, K2tog, K 4. 1 st dec.
Dec Row 3: Sl 2 WYIF, P to end.
Dec Row 4: K to end.
Next Row: Sl 2 WYIF, P to end.

Rep Dec Rows 2-4 once more. 52 (58) sts.
Switch to MC.

Rep Dec Rows 1-4 twice more. 50 (56) sts.

*Switch to C1. Rep Dec Rows 1-4 twice more. Switch to MC. Beginning with a WS row (and slipping the first 2 sts of every WS row), work in St st for 8 rows. Rep from * twice more. 44 (50) sts.

Armhole should measure 9".

Switch to C1 and beginning with a WS row (and slipping the first 2 sts of every WS row), work 5 rows in St st.

All Sizes: BO all sts.

Right Front
Place right front sts from stitch holder onto needle and join MC to wrong side.

Size 34.75" Only
Next Row (WS): P to end.
Dec Row 1 (RS): Sl 2 WYIB, K to last 4 sts, K2tog, K 2. 1 st dec.
Dec Row 2: P 2, P2tog, P to end. 1 st dec.

Rep the last two dec rows one more time. 44 sts.

Dec Row 3: Sl 2 WYIB, K to last 4 sts, K2tog, K 2. 1 st dec.
Next Row : P to end

Rep Dec Row 3 1 more time. 42 sts.
Switch to C1.

Shape Neckline
Dec Row 1 (WS): P to end
Dec Row 2 (RS): Sl 2 WYIB, K 2, SSK, K to end. 1 st dec.
Dec Row 3: P to end.
Dec Row 4: Sl 2 WYIB, K to end.
Next Row: P to end.

Rep Dec Rows 2-4 once more. 40 sts.
Switch to MC.

Rep Dec Rows 1-4 twice more. 38 sts.

*Switch to C1. Rep Dec Rows 1-4 twice more. Switch to MC. Beginning with a RS row (and slipping the first 2 sts of every RS row), work in St st for 8 rows. Rep from * once more. 34 sts.

Armhole should measure 6.5".

Switch to C1 and beginning with a RS row (and slipping the first 2 sts of every RS row), work 5 rows in St st.

Sizes 38.25" and 42" Only
Next Row (WS): P to end.
Dec Row 1 (RS): Sl 2 WYIB, K to last 4 sts, K2tog, K 2. 1 st dec.
Dec Row 2: P 2, P2tog, P to end. 1 st dec.

Rep the last two dec rows one more time. 48 (52) sts.
Dec Row 3: Sl 2 WYIB, K to last 4 sts, K2tog, K 2. 1 st dec.
Next Row: P to end.

Rep Dec Row 3 1 more time. 46 (50) sts.
Switch to C1.

Shape Neckline
Dec Row 1 (WS): P to end.
Dec Row 2 (RS): Sl 2 WYIB, K 2, SSK, K to end. 1 st dec.
Dec Row 3: P to end.

Dec Row 4: Sl 2 WYIB, K to end.
Next Row: P to end.

Rep Dec Rows 2-4 once more. 44 (48) sts.
Switch to MC.

Rep Dec Rows 1-4 twice more. 42 (46) sts.

*Switch to C1. Rep Dec Rows 1-4 twice more. Switch to MC. Beginning with a RS row (and slipping the first 2 sts of every RS row), work in St st for 8 rows. Rep from * once more. 38 (42) sts.

Then switch to C1 and beginning with a RS row (and slipping the first 2 sts of every RS row), work 8 rows in St st.

Armhole should measure 8".

Switch to MC and beginning with a RS row (and slipping the first 2 sts of every RS row), work 5 rows in St st.

Sizes 46.25" and 50" Only
Next Row (WS): P to end.
Dec Row 1 (RS): Sl 2 WYIB, K to last 4 sts, K2tog, K 2. 1 st dec.
Dec Row 2: P2, P2tog, P to end. 1 st dec.

Rep the last two dec rows one more time. 56 (62) sts.

Dec Row 3: Sl 2 WYIB, K to last 4 sts, K2tog, K 2. 1 st dec.
Next Row: P to end.

Rep Dec Row 3 1 more time. 54 (60) sts.
Switch to C1.

Shape Neckline
Dec Row 1 (WS): P to end
Dec Row 2 (RS): Sl 2 WYIB, K 2, SSK, K to end. 1 st dec.
Dec Row 3: P to end.
Dec Row 4: Sl 2 WYIB, K to end.
Next Row: P to end.

Rep Dec Rows 2-4 once more. 52 (58) sts.
Switch to MC.

Rep Dec Rows 1-4 twice more. 50 (56) sts.

*Switch to C1. Rep dec rows 1-4 twice more. Switch to MC. Beginning with a RS row (and slipping the first 2 sts of every RS row), work in St st for 8 rows. Rep from * twice more. 44 (50) sts.
Armhole should measure 9".

Switch to C1 and beginning with a RS row (and slipping the first 2 sts of every RS row), work 5 rows in St st.

All Sizes: BO all sts.

Back
Place back sts from stitch holder onto needle. Join MC with WS facing.

Size 34.75" Only
Next Row (WS): P to end.
Dec Row 1 (RS): K 3, SSK, K to last 5 sts, K2tog, K 3. 2 sts dec.
Dec Row 2: P 3, P2tog, P to last 5 sts, P2tog TBL, P 3. 2 sts dec.

Rep the last two dec rows 1 more time. 80 sts.

Dec Row 3: K 3, SSK, K to last 5 sts, K2tog, K 3. 2 sts dec.

Next Row: P to end.

Rep Dec Row 3 1 more time. 76 sts.

*Switch to C1. Beginning with a WS row, work in St st for 8 rows. Switch to MC. Beginning with a WS row, work in St st for 8 rows. Rep from * twice more.

Armhole should measure approximately 7".

Switch to C1 and beginning with a WS row work 5 rows in St st.

Sizes 38.25" and 42" Only
Next Row (WS): P to end.
Dec Row 1 (RS): K 3, SSK, K to last 5 sts, K2tog, K 3. 2 sts dec.
Dec Row 2: P 3, P3tog, P to last 5 sts, P2tog TBL, P 3. 3 sts dec.

Rep the last two dec rows 1 more time. 92 (102) sts.

Dec Row 3: K 3, SSK, K to last 5 sts, K2tog, K 3. 2 sts dec.
Next Row: P to end.

Rep Dec Row 3 1 more time. 88 (98) sts.

*Switch to C1. Beginning with a WS row, work in St st for 8 rows. Switch to MC. Beginning with a WS row, work in St st for 8 rows. Rep from * twice more.

Then switch to C1 and beginning with a WS row work 8 rows in St st.

Armhole should measure 8".

Then switch to MC and beginning with a WS row work 5 rows in St st.

Sizes 46.25" and 50 Only
Next Row (WS): P to end.
Dec Row 1 (RS): K 3, SSK, K to last 5 sts, K2tog, K 3. 2 sts dec.
Dec Row 2: P 3, P3tog, P to last 5 sts, P2tog TBL, P 3. 3 sts dec.

Rep the last two dec rows 1 more time. 116 (122) sts.

Dec Row 3: K 3, SSK, K to last 5 sts, K2tog, K 3. 2 sts dec.
Dec Row 4: P to end.

Rep Dec Row 3 1 more time. 112 (118) sts.

Switch to C1 and work Dec Row 4 once more and then work Dec Rows 3 and 4 once more. 110 (116) sts.

Beginning with a RS row work 5 rows in St st.

*Switch to MC. Beginning with a WS row, work in St st for 8 rows. Switch to C1. Beginning with a WS row, work in St st for 8 rows. Rep from * twice more.

Then switch to MC and beginning with a WS row work 8 rows in St st.

Armhole should measure 9".

Then switch to C1 and beginning with a WS row work 5 rows in St st.

All Sizes: BO all sts.

Finishing
Sew left and right shoulders to the top edges of back as follows

(for each shoulder); sew 1 (1, 1, 1)", make 0.25 (0.25, 0.5, 0.5, 0.75)" gather of the front piece, sew 0.75 (0.75, 0.75, 0.75, 0.75)", make 0.25 (0.5, 0.5, 0.5, 0.75)" gather of the front piece, sew 0.5 (0.5, 0.5, 0.5, 0.5)", make 0.25 (0.25, 0.5, 0.75, 0.75)" gather of the front piece, sew 0.5 (0.5, 0.5, 0.5, 0.5)", make 0.25 (0.5, 0.5, 0.5, 0.75)" gather of the front piece, sew 0.75 (0.75, 0.75, 0.75, 0.75)", make 0.25 (0.25, 0.5, 0.5, 0.75)" gather of the front piece, sew 1 (1, 1, 1, 1)".

Weave in all ends.

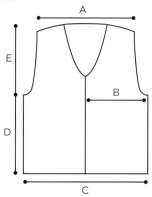

A 12.75 (14.75, 16.25, 18.25, 19.25)"
B 8.75 (9.5, 10.5, 11.5, 12.5)"
C 34.75 (38.25, 42, 46.25, 50)"
D 12 (12, 12, 14, 14)"
E 7 (8.5, 8.5, 9.5, 9.5)"

STILETTO PULLOVER

by Kristen TenDyke

FINISHED MEASUREMENTS
35 (38, 41.25, 44.25, 47.25, 50.25, 53.25)" finished bust measurement; garment is meant to be worn with 0–2" of positive ease

YARN
Knit Picks Swish DK (100% Superwash Merino Wool; 123 yards/50g): Amethyst Heather 24310, 7 (7, 8, 8, 9, 10, 10) balls

NEEDLES
US 5 (3.75mm) 32" circular needles plus a set of 4 or 5 DPNs, or size to obtain gauge

NOTIONS
Yarn Needle
Stitch Markers
Scrap Yarn or Stitch Holder

GAUGE
21 sts and 29 rows/rnds = 4" in St st in the rnd and worked flat, blocked

Stiletto Pullover

Notes:

The sleeves and body are knit separately in the round from the bottom up to the underarms, where they are joined. The yoke is knit from the bottom up, decreasing the body and sleeves along raglan lines. The underarm stitches are joined using the Three-Needle Bind-Off Method once the sweater is complete.

When working the chart, read all rows from right to left, as RS rows.

P1, K1 Ribbing (worked in the rnd over a multiple of 2 sts)
All Rnds: *P1, K1; rep from * around.

Stockinette Stitch (worked in the rnd)
Rnd 1: Knit.
Rep Rnd 1 for pattern.

Stockinette Stitch (worked flat)
Row 1 (RS): Knit.
Row 2 (WS): Purl.
Rep Rows 1 and 2 for pattern.

Stiletto Pattern (worked in the rnd over a multiple of 20 sts plus 11)
Rnd 1: P1, YO, SSK, K2tog, YO, K1, YO, SSK, K2tog, YO, P1, *SSK, K2, YO, K1, YO, K2, K2tog, P1, YO, SSK, K2tog, YO, K1, YO, SSK, K2tog, YO, P1; rep from * to M.
Rnd 2 and all even numbered rnds through Rnd 16: P1, *K9, K1; rep from * to M.
Rnd 3: P1, K1, YO, SSK, K3, K2tog, YO, K1, P1, *SSK, K2, YO, K1, YO, K2, K2tog, P1, K1, YO, SSK, K3, K2tog, YO, K1, P1; rep from * to M.
Rnd 5: P1, K2, YO, SSK, K1, K2tog, YO, K2, P1, *SSK, K2, YO, K1, YO, K2, K2tog, P1, K2, YO, SSK, K1, K2tog, YO, K2, P1; rep from * to M.
Rnd 7: P1, K3, YO, SK2P, YO, K3, P1, *SSK, K2, YO, K1, YO, K2, K2tog, P1, K3, YO, SK2P, YO, K3, P1; rep from * to M.
Rnd 9: P1, SSK, K2, YO, K1, YO, K2, K2tog, P1, *YO, SSK, K2tog, YO, K1, YO, SSK, K2tog, YO, P1, SSK, K2, YO, K1, YO, K2, K2tog, P1; rep from * to M.
Rnd 11: P1, SSK, K2, YO, K1, YO, K2, K2tog, P1, *K1, YO, SSK, K3, K2tog, YO, K1, P1, SSK, K2, YO, K1, YO, K2, K2tog, P1; rep from * to M.
Rnd 13: P1, SSK, K2, YO, K1, YO, K2, P1, *K2, YO, SSK, K1, K2tog, YO, K2, P1, SSK, K2, YO, K1, YO, K2, K2tog, P1; rep from * to M.
Rnd 15: P1, SSK, K2, YO, K1, YO, K2, K2tog, P1, *K3, YO, SK2P, YO, K3, P1, SSK, K2, YO, K1, YO, K2, K2tog, P1; rep from * to M.
Rep Rnds 1–16 for pattern.

Three Needle Bind-Off Method: Hold 2 DPNs parallel with an equal number of sts on each DPN, and the RSs together (to form ridge on inside of garment). With a third needle, K the first st of front and back needles together, *K next st from each needle together (2 sts on right needle), BO 1 st; rep from * until all sts are BO.

DIRECTIONS

Sleeves (make two the same)
The sleeves are worked in the rnd from the cuff to the underarm.

Cuff
With DPNs, CO 62 (66, 70, 74, 78, 82, 86) sts. PM for beginning of rnd and join to work in the rnd, being careful not to twist sts.

Work in P1, K1 Ribbing for 1".

Shape Sleeve
Begin working in St st, while working increases at each end of the rnd as follows:
Inc Rnd: K1, M1L, K to last st, M1R, K1. 2 sts inc.
Knit 7 rnds.

Rep the last 8 rnds 2 more times. 68 (72, 76, 80, 84, 88, 92) sts.

Continue working in St st until sleeve measures 5" from beginning.

Divide for Underarm
Break yarn. Place the last 3 (4, 5, 6, 7, 8, 9) sts and the first 4 (5, 6, 7, 8, 9, 10) sts onto a stitch holder or scrap yarn, removing the M. 61 (63, 65, 67, 69, 71, 73) sts remain. Place remaining sts onto a piece of scrap yarn for yoke and set aside.

Body
The body is knit in the rnd from the lower hem to the underarm.

Hem
With circular needle, CO 184 (200, 216, 232, 248, 264, 280) sts. PM for beginning of rnd and join to work in the rnd, being careful not to twist sts.

Work in P1, K1 Ribbing for 1".
Knit 1 rnd.

Establish Pattern
It is recommended to use two different colored stitch markers to easily identify the Side or Stiletto Pattern markers apart.

Next Rnd: K20 (24, 18, 22, 26, 20, 24), PM for Stiletto Pattern, work 51 (51, 71, 71, 71, 91, 91) sts in Stiletto Pattern, PM for Stiletto Pattern, K21 (25, 19, 23, 27, 21, 25), PM for side, K20 (24, 18, 22, 26, 20, 24), PM for Stiletto Pattern, work 51 (51, 71, 71, 71, 91, 91) sts in Stiletto Pattern, PM, K21 (25, 19, 23, 27, 21, 25) to end.
Work 1 more rnd as established.

Shape Waist
Continue working in pattern as established while working waist and bust shaping as follows:
Dec Rnd: K2, K2tog, work as established to 4 sts before side M, SSK, K2, SM, K2, K2tog, work as established to last 4 sts, SSK, K2. 4 sts dec.

Work 11 rnds even as established.

Rep the last 12 rnds 4 more times. 164 (180, 196, 212, 228, 244, 260) sts remain.

Shape Bust
Inc Rnd: K2, M1L, work as established to 2 sts before side M, M1R, K2, SM, K2, M1L, work as established to last 2 sts, M1R, K2. 4 sts inc.

Work 9 rnds even as established.

Rep the last 10 rnds 4 more times. 184 (200, 216, 232, 248, 264, 280) sts.

Continue working even as established until body measures approximately 17.5" from CO edge or desired length to underarm, ending after Rnd 7 of Stiletto Pattern.

Divide for Underarms

Next Rnd: K3 (4, 5, 6, 7, 8, 9), place the 3 (4, 5, 6, 7, 8, 9) sts just worked and the 4 (5, 6, 7, 8, 9, 10) sts before the beginning of rnd M onto a stitch holder or scrap yarn removing the M, work as established to side M removing the Stiletto Pattern markers as you come to them, K3 (4, 5, 6, 7, 8, 9), place the 3 (4, 5, 6, 7, 8, 9) sts just worked and the 4 (5, 6, 7, 8, 9, 10) sts before the side M onto a stitch holder or scrap yarn removing the M, work to end as established, removing the Stiletto Pattern markers as you come to them. 85 (91, 97, 103, 109, 115, 121) sts remain each front and back.

Yoke

On the next rnd the sleeves and body are joined together on the circular needle. All sts are now worked in St st.

Joining Rnd: Return 61 (63, 65, 67, 69, 71, 73) held sleeve sts to DPNs and use the circular needle to knit across, PM for raglan, K85 (91, 97, 103, 109, 115, 121) front sts, PM for raglan, return 61 (63, 65, 67, 69, 71, 73) held sleeve sts to DPNs and knit across, PM for raglan, K85 (91, 97, 103, 109, 115, 121) back sts, PM for beginning of rnd. 292 (308, 324, 340, 356, 372, 388) sts.

Shape Raglan

Sizes - (-, 41.25, 44.25, 47.25, 50.25, 53.25)" Only:
Body and Sleeve Dec Rnd: *K1, K2tog, K across sleeve to 3 sts before next M, SSK, K1, SM, K2tog, K across body to 2 sts before next M, SSK, SM; rep from * once more. 8 sts dec.

Knit 1 rnd.

Body Dec Rnd: *K across sleeve to next M, SM, K2tog, K across body to 2 sts before next M, SSK, SM; rep from * once more. 4 sts dec.

Knit 1 rnd.

Rep the last 4 rnds - (-, 0, 1, 2, 2, 3) more times. - (-, 312, 316, 320, 336, 340) sts remain; - (-, 63, 63, 63, 65, 65) sts each sleeve and - (-, 93, 95, 97, 103, 105) sts each back and front.

All Sizes

Body and Sleeve Dec Rnd: *K1, K2tog, K across sleeve to 3 sts before next M, SSK, K1, SM, K2tog, K across body to 2 sts before next M, SSK, SM; rep from * once more. 8 sts dec.

Knit 1 rnd.

Rep the last 2 rnds 5 (6, 6, 5, 5, 4, 4) more times. 244 (252, 256, 268, 272, 296, 300) sts remain; 49 (49, 49, 51, 51, 55, 55) sts each sleeve and 73 (77, 79, 83, 85, 93, 95) sts each back and front.

Body and Sleeve Dec Rnd: *K1, K2tog, K across sleeve to 3 sts before next M, SSK, K1, SM, K2tog, K across body to 2 sts before next M, SSK, SM; rep from * once more. 8 sts dec.
Body Dec Rnd: *K across sleeve to next M, SM, K2tog, K across body to 2 sts before next M, SSK, SM; rep from * once more. 4 sts dec.

Rep the last 2 rnds 5 (6, 6, 7, 7, 9, 9) more times. 172 (168, 172, 172, 176, 176, 180) sts remain; 37 (35, 35, 35, 35, 35, 35) sts each sleeve and 49 (49, 51, 51, 53, 53, 55) sts each back and front.

Shape Front Neck

Body and Sleeve Dec Rnd: K1, K2tog, K across sleeve to 3 sts before next M, SSK, K1, SM, K2tog, K11, BO 23 (23, 25, 25, 27, 27, 29) sts, K11 to 2 sts before next M, SSK, SM, K1, K2tog, K across sleeve to 3 sts before next M, SSK, K1, SM, K2tog, K to last 2 sts, SSK. 141 (137, 139, 139, 141, 141, 143) sts remain; 12 sts each front, 35 (33, 33, 33, 33, 33, 33) sts each sleeve and 47 (47, 49, 49, 51, 51, 53) sts for back.

Break yarn. Slip 47 (45, 45, 45, 45, 45, 45) sts from left needle to right needle until both needle tips are at the center front BO sts. Rejoin yarn preparing to work a WS row. Cont working back and forth in rows, in St st.

Body Dec Row (WS): *P to 2 sts before M, P2tog, SM, P across sleeve to next M, SM, SSP; rep from * once more, P to end. 4 sts dec.
Neck, Body and Sleeve Dec Row (RS): K1, K2tog, *K to 2 sts before M, SSK, SM, K1, K2tog, K across sleeve to 3 sts before next M, SSK, K1, SM, K2tog; rep from * once more, K to last 3 sts, SSK, K1. 10 sts dec.

Rep the last 2 rows 1 (2, 2, 2, 2, 2, 2) more times, then rep Body Dec Row once more on a WS row. 109 (91, 93, 93, 95, 95, 97) sts remain; 5 (2, 2, 2, 2, 2, 2) sts each front, 31 (27, 27, 27, 27, 27, 27) sts each sleeve and 37 (33, 35, 37, 37, 39) sts for back.

Size 35 (-, -, -, -, -, -)" Only
Next Row (RS): Rep Neck, Body and Sleeve Dec Row. 99 sts remain; 3 sts each front, 29 sts each sleeve and 35 sts for back.

Body and Sleeve Dec Row (WS): *P to 2 sts before M, P2tog, SM, P1, SSP, P across sleeve to 3 sts before next M, P2tog, P1, SM, SSP; rep from * once more, P to end. 91 sts remain; 2 sts each front, 27 sts each sleeve and 33 sts for back.

All Sizes
BO all sts loosely.

Finishing

Neckband: With RS facing and circular needle, begin at center of back neck, PU and K 1 st in each BO st to front neck, 2 sts for every 3 rows along selvedge edge to front neck BO sts, 1 st in each front neck BO st, 2 sts for every 3 rows along selvedge edge, then 1 st in each BO st to center back, being careful to finish with an even number of sts (Note: If necessary, decrease 1 st by K2tog at the end of the following rnd.)

Work P1, K1 Ribbing for 1".

BO all sts loosely in pattern.

Join Underarms: With WSs facing, slip 7 (9, 11, 13, 15, 17, 19) held underarm sts onto DPNs, picking up 1 additional st at each end of needle. 9 (11, 13, 15, 17, 19, 21) sts on each DPN. Hold the needles parallel with RSs facing together and use the Three-Needle Bind Off Method to BO the sts together. Rep for second underarm.

Weave in ends, wash and block to diagram.

Legend

●	**purl**	purl stitch
O	**yo**	Yarn Over
\	**ssk**	Slip one stitch as if to knit, slip another stitch as if to knit. Insert left-hand needle into front of these 2 stitches and knit them together
/	**k2tog**	Knit two stitches together as one stitch
☐	**knit**	knit stitch
⅄	**sl1 k2tog psso**	slip 1, k2tog, pass slip stitch over k2tog
☐	**pattern repeat**	

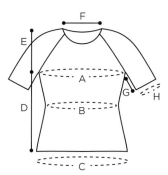

A 35 (38, 41.25, 44.25, 47.25, 50.25, 53.25)"
B 31.25 (34.25, 37.25, 40.5, 43.5, 46.5, 49.5)"
C 35 (38, 41.25, 44.25, 50.25, 53.25)"
D 17.5"
E 7 (7.5, 8.25, 8.75, 9.25, 9.5, 10)"
F 6.25 (6.25, 6.75, 6.75, 7, 7, 7.25)"
G 5"
H 11.75 (12.5, 13.25, 14, 14.75, 15.5, 16.5)"

Stiletto Chart

31	30	29	28	27	26	25	24	23	22	21	20	19	18	17	16	15	14	13	12	11	10	9	8	7	6	5	4	3	2	1	
●										●										●										●	16
●	/			O		O			\	●				O	⅄	O				●	/			O		O			\	●	15
●										●										●										●	14
●	/			O		O			\	●			O	/			\	O		●	/			O		O			\	●	13
●										●										●										●	12
●	/			O		O			\	●		O	/					\	O	●	/			O		O			\	●	11
●										●										●										●	10
●	/			O		O			\	●	O	/	\	O		O	/	\	O	●	/			O		O			\	●	9
●										●										●										●	8
●				O	⅄	O				●	/			O		O				●				O	⅄	O				●	7
●										●										●										●	6
●		O	/		\	O				●	/			O		O				●		O	/		\	O				●	5
●										●										●										●	4
●		O	/				\	O		●	/			O		O				●		O	/				\	O		●	3
●										●										●										●	2
●	O	/	\	O		O	/	\	O	●	/			O		O				●	O	/	\	O		O	/	\	O	●	1

SPRING THAW CARDIGAN

by Kephren Pritchett

FINISHED MEASUREMENTS

33 (37, 41, 45, 49, 53, 57, 61, 65)" finished bust measurement (buttoned); garment is meant to be worn with 0 to 3" of positive ease

YARN

Knit Picks Comfy Fingering (75% Pima Cotton, 25% Acrylic; 218 yards/50g): Sea Foam 24828, 5 (6, 6, 7, 8, 8, 9, 9, 10) skeins

NEEDLES

US 4 (3.5mm) circular needles and DPNs or two 24" circular needles for two circulars technique, or one 32" or longer circular needle for Magic Loop technique, or size to obtain gauge

US 2 (3mm) circular needles and DPNs or two 24" circular needles for two circulars technique, or one 32" or longer circular needle for Magic Loop technique, or size to obtain gauge

NOTIONS

Yarn Needle
Stitch Markers
Scrap Yarn or Stitch Holders
12 (12, 12, 13, 13, 13, 14, 14, 14) 0.5" buttons

GAUGE

24 sts and 32 rows = 4" in St st on larger needles, blocked
22 sts and 44 rows = 4" in Garter st on smaller needles, blocked
10 sts and 8 rows = 1.75" wide x 1" tall over one chart pattern rep on larger needles, blocked

Spring Thaw Cardigan

Notes:

The cardigan is worked from the top down beginning at the shoulders. The back is worked first to the underarms, then stitches are picked up for each front and worked to the underarms. Fronts and back are joined and worked in one piece to the Garter stitch hem. Sleeve stitches are picked up from the armholes, shaped with short rows, and worked in the round to the Garter st cuff. Stitches are picked up from the fronts and neck and worked in Garter stitch for the button bands and neck edge.

Stockinette st (St st worked flat or in the rnd over any number of sts)
Row 1: Knit.
Row 2: Purl.
Repeat Rows 1-2 to work flat. To work in the rnd, knit all rnds.

Garter Stitch (worked flat or in the rnd over any number of sts)
Rnd 1: Knit.
Rnd 2: Purl.
Rep Rnds 1-2 to work in the rnd. To work flat, knit all rows.

Falling Leaves Pattern (worked flat over multiple of 10 sts plus 1)
Row 1 (RS): K3, K2tog, YO, K1, YO, SSK, K3.
Row 2, 4, and 6 (WS): Purl.
Row 3: K2, K2tog, (K1, YO) twice, K1, SSK, K2.
Row 5: K1, K2tog, K2, YO, K1, YO, K2, SSK, K1.
Row 7: K2tog, K3, YO, K1, YO, K3, SSK.
Row 8: P to 5 sts before M, PM, (P to m, RM) twice, P5, PM.
Row 9: K3, K2tog, YO, *K1, YO, SSK, K5, K2tog, YO; rep from * to 6 sts before M, K1, YO, SSK, K3.
Row 10, 12, and 14: Purl.
Row 11: K2, K2tog, K1, YO, *K1, YO, K1, SSK, K3, K2tog, K1, YO; rep from * to 6 sts before M, K1, YO, K1, SSK, K2.
Row 13: K1, K2tog, K2, YO, *K1, YO, K2, SSK, K1, K2tog, K2, YO; rep from * to 6 sts before M, K1, YO, K2, SSK, K1.
Row 15: K2tog, K3, YO, *K1, YO, K3, Sk2p, K3, YO; rep from * to 6 sts before M, K1, YO, K3, SSK.
Rep Rows 8—15 for pattern.

German Short Rows
Make Double Stitch (DS): Sl1 P-wise WYIF, pull yarn up over the needle and to the back. On return rows, work both strands of the DS as a single stitch.

Twisted Purl CO
P1, but do not remove st from LH needle. Twist RH needle to the back to place front loop of new stitch onto back of LH needle.

DIRECTIONS
Body
Back
With larger needle CO 81 (85, 87, 91, 93, 95, 99, 105, 107) sts.

Next Row (WS): Purl.
Short Row 1 (RS): K62, (66, 68, 71, 73, 75, 78, 84, 85) turn.
Short Row 2 (WS): Make DS, P 42 (46, 48, 50, 52, 54, 56, 62, 62), turn.
Short Row 3: Make DS, K to DS, K DS as single st, K3, turn.
Short Row 4: Make DS, P to DS, P DS as single st, P3, turn.

Rep the last 2 rows 2 (3, 3, 4, 4, 4, 5, 5, 5) more times.

Next Row: Make DS, K to end.
Setup Lace Pattern (WS): P35 (37, 38, 40, 41, 42, 44, 47, 48), PM, P11, PM, P to DS, P DS, P to end.
WE in St st for 12 (10, 6, 6, 0, 4, 2, 4, 0) rows.
Next Row (RS): K to M, SM, work from Falling Leaves Chart to M, SM, K to end.
Cont in St st and working Falling Leaves Chart between markers for a total of 32 (36, 34, 38, 42, 34, 36, 32, 32) rows.

Shape Armhole
Inc Row (RS): K2, M1L, K to M, SM, work Falling Leaves Chart to M, SM, K to last 2 sts, M1R, K2. 2 sts inc.
Next Row (WS): Purl.
Rep the last 2 rows 3 (5, 10, 10, 12, 16, 17, 19, 23) more times. 89 (97, 109, 113, 119, 129, 135, 145, 155) sts. Transfer back sts to a holder.

Right Front
With RS facing and larger needle, working from shoulder to neck, PU and K 22 (22, 22, 23, 23, 23, 24, 24, 25) sts for right shoulder from right side of back cast-on edge

Short Row 1 (WS): P3, turn.
Short Row 2 (RS): Make DS, K to end.
Short Row 3: P to DS, P DS as single st, P3, turn.
Short Row 4: Make DS, K to end.
Rep the last 2 rows 2 (3, 3, 4, 4, 4, 5, 5, 5) more times.
Next Row (WS): P to DS, purl DS as single st, P to end.
WE in St st for 14 rows.

Shape Front Neck
Inc Row (RS): K to last 2 sts, M1R, K 2. 1 st inc.
Next Row: Purl.

Rep the last 2 rows 2 (2, 2, 3, 3, 3, 4, 4, 4) more times. 25 (25, 25, 27, 27, 27, 29, 29, 30) sts.
Knit 1 row.
Neck CO: Using the Twisted Purl CO, CO 17 (19, 20, 20, 21, 22, 22, 25, 25) onto LH needle. 42 (44, 45, 47, 48, 49, 51, 54, 55) sts.
WE in St st for 23 (25, 19, 21, 19, 15, 13, 11, 7) rows, ending with a WS row.

Shape Armhole
Inc Row (RS): K2, M1L, K to end. 1 st inc.
Next Row (WS): Purl.
Rep the last 2 rows 3 (5, 10, 10, 12, 16, 17, 19, 23) more times. 46 (50, 56, 58, 61, 66, 69, 74, 79) sts.

Left Front
With RS facing and larger needle, working from neck to shoulder, PU and K 22 (22, 22, 23, 23, 23, 24, 24, 25) sts for left shoulder from left side of back cast-on edge.

Purl 1 row.
Short Row 1 (RS): K3, turn.
Short Row 2 (WS): Make DS, P to end.
Short Row 3: K to DS, K DS as single st, K3, turn.
Short Row 4: Make DS, P to end.
Rep the last 2 rows 2 (3, 3, 4, 4, 4, 5, 5, 5) more times.
Next Row: K to DS, K DS as single st, K to end.
WE in St st for 13 rows.

Shape Front Neck

Inc Row (RS): K2, M1L, K to end. 1 st inc.

Next Row: Purl.

Rep the last 2 rows 2 (2, 2, 3, 3, 4, 4, 4) more times. 25 (25, 25, 27, 27, 27, 29, 29, 30) sts.

Neck CO: Using the Twisted Purl CO, CO 17 (19, 20, 20, 21, 22, 22, 25, 25) onto LH needle, 42 (44, 45, 47, 48, 49, 51, 54, 55) sts. WE in St st for 24 (26, 20, 22, 20, 16, 14, 12, 8) rows, ending with a WS row.

Shape Armhole

Inc Row (RS): K to last 2 sts, M1R, K2, 1 st inc.

Next Row (WS): Purl.

Repeat the last 2 rows 3 (5, 10, 10, 12, 16, 17, 19, 23) more times. 46 (50, 56, 58, 61, 66, 69, 74, 79) sts.

Join Fronts to Back

K left front sts, turn and using the Twisted Purl CO, CO 6 (10, 10, 18, 24, 26, 32, 34, 36) sts for underarm, turn and K back sts to M, work Falling Leaves Pattern to M, K to end of back sts, turn and using the Twisted Purl CO, CO 6 (10, 10, 18, 24, 26, 32, 34, 36) sts for underarm, turn and K right front sts. 193 (217, 241, 265, 289, 313, 337, 361, 385) sts.

Cont in St st and working Falling Leaves Pattern between markers for 112 (112, 112, 116, 116, 116, 120, 120, 120) more rows, ending with a RS row.

Change to smaller needle and work 4 rows in Garter st. BO on WS.

Sleeve Caps

With smaller needle and beginning at the center of the underarm CO with RS facing, PU and K 64 (74, 78, 90, 98, 104, 112, 116, 122) sts, (1 st for each st from underarm CO, 1 st for every 2 rows at armhole edge, and 2 sts for every 3 rows 4 times from top of sleeve) placing a marker after 32 (37, 39, 45, 49, 52, 56, 58, 61) sts. PM for beginning of rnd. Change to larger needle.

Short Row 1 (RS): K to M, SM, K 8, (9, 10, 10, 11, 13, 13, 14, 15), turn.

Short Row 2 (WS): Make DS, P 15, (17, 19, 19, 21, 25, 25, 27, 29), turn.

Short Row 3: Make DS, K to DS, K DS as single st, K 1, turn.

Short Row 4: Make DS, P to DS, P DS as single st, P 1, turn.

Rep the last 2 rows 19 (21, 22, 24, 24, 24, 25, 25, 26) more times.

Next Row: K to DS, K DS as single st, K to end.

Sleeves

WE in St st in the rnd for 16 (12, 14, 10, 13, 20, 28, 27, 21) rnds.

Dec Rnd: K3 (5, 5, 9, 12, 13, 16, 17, 18) SSK, K to last 5 (7, 7, 11, 14, 15, 18, 19, 20) sts, K2tog, K to end. 2 sts dec.

Rep Dec Rnd every 15 (11, 11, 8, 7, 6, 5, 5, 5)th rnd 8 (12, 12, 17, 19, 21, 24, 25, 27) more times. 46 (48, 52, 54, 58, 60, 62, 64, 66) sts.

Work 4 rnds Garter st. BO P-wise.

Button Band

With RS facing and smaller needle PU and K 101 (103, 105, 111, 113, 113, 119, 119, 121) sts from Left Front.

Work 4 rows in Garter st. BO on WS.

Buttonhole Band

With RS facing and smaller needle PU and K 101 (103, 105, 111, 113, 113, 119, 119, 121) sts from Right Front.

Next Row (WS): Knit.

Buttonhole Row: K2 (4, 6, 3, 5, 5, 2, 2, 4) *K2tog, YO, K7; rep from * to end. 11 (11, 11, 12, 12, 12, 13, 13, 13) button holes.

Work 2 more rows in Garter st. BO on WS.

Neck Band

With RS facing and smaller needle PU and K3 sts from top of Buttonhole Band, PU and K 17 (19, 20, 20, 21, 22, 22, 25, 25) sts from Right Front CO, PU and K 20 (21, 21, 24, 24, 24, 27, 27, 27) sts from right side edge, PU and K 37 (41, 43, 45, 47, 49, 51, 57, 57) sts from back neck, PU and K 20 (21, 21, 24, 24, 24, 27, 27, 27) sts from left side edge, PU and K 17 (19, 20, 20, 21, 22, 22, 25, 25) sts from Left Front CO, PU and K 3 sts from top of Button Band. 117 (127, 131, 139, 143, 147, 155, 167, 167) sts.

Work 4 rows in Garter st. BO on WS.

Finishing

Weave in ends, sew on buttons opposite button holes, wash and block to measurements.

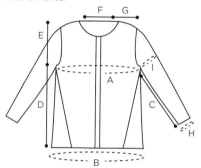

A 33 (37, 41, 45, 49, 53, 57, 61, 65)"
B 34.75 (38.75, 42.75, 46.75, 51, 55, 59, 63, 67)"
C 17.5 (18.5, 18.75, 18.75, 18.75, 18.75, 19, 19.5, 20)"
D 14.5 (14.5, 14.5, 15, 15, 15, 15.5, 15.5, 15.5)"
E 6.75 (7.5, 8, 8.5, 8.75, 9.25, 9.5, 9.75, 10.25)"
F 6.25 (7, 7.25, 7.5, 8, 8.25, 8.5, 9.5, 9.5)"
G 3.75 (3.75, 3.75, 3.75, 3.75, 3.75, 4, 4, 4.25)"
H 7.75 (8, 8.75, 9, 9.75, 10, 10.25, 10.75, 11)"
I 10.75 (12.25, 13, 15, 16.25, 17.25, 18.75, 19.25, 20.25)"

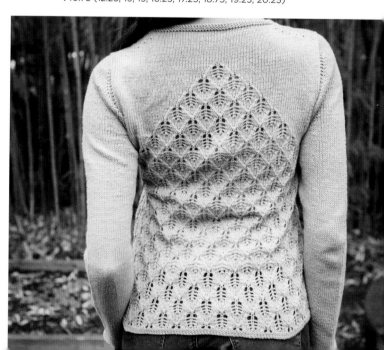

WHITWELL TOP

by Kate Heppell

FINISHED MEASUREMENTS

36 (39.5, 43, 46.75, 50.25, 53.75, 57.25, 61, 65.5)" finished bust measurement, garment is meant to be worn with 3" of positive ease

YARN

Knit Picks Shine Sport (60% Pima Cotton, 40% Modal; 110 yards/50g): Cosmopolitan 25344, 7 (7, 8, 9, 10, 10, 11, 12, 13) balls

NEEDLES

US 4 (3.5mm) straight or 24" or longer circular needles, or size to obtain gauge

NOTIONS

Yarn Needle
4 Lockable Stitch Markers
Stitch Holder

GAUGE

18 sts and 30 rows = 4" in Whitwell Pattern, blocked

Whitwell Top

Notes:

This top is worked entirely flat and features an all-over pattern which can be worked either from the chart or the written instructions, whichever you prefer. The front and back are knitted separately and then joined at one shoulder. Stitches are picked up around the neckline and worked in garter st for the collar. The other shoulder is then joined. Stitches are picked up along the sides to work the armhole edge before the sides are sewn up.

When working the chart, read RS rows (odd numbers) from right to left, and WS rows (even numbers) from left to right.

Whitwell Pattern (worked over a multiple of 8 sts plus 1 st)
Rows 1-7: Knit.
Rows 8, 10, 12, 14 (WS): Purl.
Row 9 (RS): *K1, YO, SSK, K3, K2tog, YO; rep from * to last st, K1.
Row 11: *K2, YO, SSK, K1, K2tog, YO, K1; rep from * to last st, K1.
Row 13: *K3, YO, CDD, YO, K2; rep from * to last st, K1.
Rep Rows 1-14 for pattern.

DIRECTIONS

Back

CO 81 (89, 97, 105, 113, 121, 129, 137, 145) sts.
Work Rows 1-14 of Whitwell Pattern from chart or written instructions for 126 (123, 119, 114, 111, 107, 103, 100, 96) rows.
Place a lockable stitch marker at each end of the last row worked.
Cont working in Whitwell Pattern for 48 (51, 55, 60, 63, 67, 71, 74, 78) more rows.
BO.

Front

Work as for Back through placement of stitch marker.
Cont working in Whitwell pattern for 14 (17, 21, 26, 29, 33, 37, 40, 44) more rows.
You should be finishing after a Row 14 of the Whitwell pattern.

Right Shoulder

Next Row (RS): K24 (27, 29, 32, 35, 37, 40, 43, 45), K3tog, place the remaining 54 (59, 65, 70, 75, 81, 86, 91, 97) sts onto a stitch holder.
Working in Garter st (K all rows), K3tog at neck edge on next row.
Cont in Garter st, K2tog at neck edge on each of next 4 rows.
On the remaining 19 (22, 24, 27, 30, 32, 35, 38, 40) sts, starting with Row 7, cont in Whitwell Pattern for 28 more rows.
BO.

Left Shoulder

Leave center 27 (29, 33, 35, 37, 41, 43, 45, 49) sts on holder for neck and return remaining 27 (30, 32, 35, 38, 40, 43, 46, 48) sts to needles, ready to work a RS row.
Work the same as Left Shoulder, reversing all shaping.
BO.

Collar

Sew Left Shoulder seam using Mattress Stitch.
Using Front as a guide, place a lockable stitch marker to indicate the point where the Back Neck will join the Right Front Neck.
With RS facing and starting at Back Neck marker, PU and K 43 (45, 49, 51, 53, 57, 59, 61, 65) sts along back neck, PU and K 20 sts along left front neck, K all sts from stitch holder, PU and K 20 sts along right front neck. 110 (114, 122, 126, 130, 138, 142, 146, 154) sts.
Knit 10 rows.
BO.
Sew Right Shoulder Seam using Mattress Stitch, up through the Collar rows.

Sleeves (work both the same)

With RS facing, PU and K 56 (60, 66, 72, 76, 80, 84, 88, 92) sts between side markers.
Knit 20 rows.
BO.

Finishing

Sew side seams from CO through Sleeves, using Mattress Stitch.
Weave in ends, wash and block to diagram.

Whitwell Pattern Chart

	9	8	7	6	5	4	3	2	1	
14										
				O	∧	O				13
12										
			O	/		\	O			11
10										
		O	/				\	O		9
8										
										7
6	●	●	●	●	●	●	●	●	●	
										5
4	●	●	●	●	●	●	●	●	●	
										3
2	●	●	●	●	●	●	●	●	●	
										1

Legend

knit
RS: knit stitch
WS: purl stitch
☐

purl
RS: purl stitch
WS: knit stitch
●

yo
yarn over
O

ssk
Slip one stitch as if to knit, slip another stitch as if to knit. Insert left-hand needle into front of these 2 stitches and knit them together

k2tog
Knit two stitches together as one stitch

Central Double Dec
Slip first and second stitches together as if to knit. Knit 1 stitch. Pass two slipped stitches over the knit stitch.

☐ **pattern repeat**

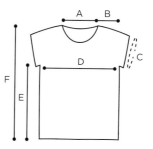

A 9.5 (10, 11, 11.25, 11.75, 12.75, 13, 13.5, 14.5)"
B 4.25 (5, 5.25, 6, 6.75, 7, 7.75, 8.5, 9)"
C 6.5 (6.75, 7.25, 8, 8.5, 9, 9.5, 10, 10.5)"
D 18 (19.75, 21.5, 23.25, 25, 27, 28.75, 30.5, 32.25)"
E 16.75 (16.5, 15.75, 15.25, 14.75, 14.25, 13.75, 13.25, 12.75)"
F 23.25"

GOLDEN GARDENS PULLOVER

by Allison Griffith

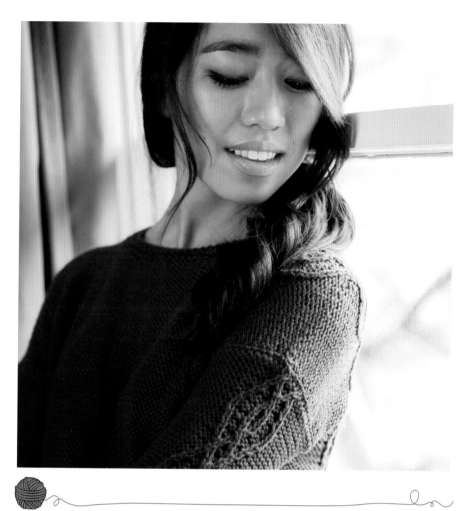

FINISHED MEASUREMENTS

35 (38.75, 43.25, 46.75, 50.5, 55, 58.5, 62, 66.5, 70.25)" finished bust measurement; garment is meant to be worn with 8-10" of ease

YARN

Knit Picks Comfy Worsted (75% Pima Cotton, 25% Acrylic; 109 yards/50g): Celestial 25314, 9 (9, 10, 10, 11, 11, 12, 12, 13, 14)

NEEDLES

US 9 (5.5mm) straight or circular needles, or size to obtain gauge and a 16" circular needle or dpns

NOTIONS

Yarn Needle
Stitch Markers
Cable Needle
Scrap yarn or stitch holder

GAUGE

17.75 sts and 22.25 rows = 4" in rev st st, blocked

Golden Gardens Pullover

Notes:

This sweater is knit flat in pieces, then seamed. The front and back are joined with the Kitchener stitch at the shoulders. The sleeves are sewn in place, centered at the shoulders. The sleeves, underarms, and body sides are sewn closed, leaving the split hem open. Then, a simple neckband is picked up and knit in the round, before being bound off loosely purlwise.

Reverse Stockinette Stitch (worked flat over any number of sts)
Row 1 (RS): P.
Row 2 (WS): K.

Kitchener Stitch
Follow the instructions provided on the Knit Picks website here:
http://tutorials.knitpicks.com/wptutorials/kitchener-stitch/

Sewn Bind Off (optional)
Follow the instructions provided on the Knit Picks website here:
http://tutorials.knitpicks.com/wptutorials/sewn-bind-off/

DIRECTIONS

Back
The back is worked flat from the hem up.

Split Hem
Loosely CO 78 (86, 96, 104, 112, 122, 130, 138, 148, 156) sts. K 5 rows.
Set-Up Row: K 8 (11, 16, 19, 22, 26, 28, 32, 35, 38), PM, K3, P2, K2, P2, K3, PM, K to end.
Row 1 (RS): K4, P to M, SM, work Golden Gardens Chart, SM, P to 4 before end, K4.
Row 2 (WS): K to M, SM, work Golden Gardens Chart, SM, K to end.

Repeat the last two rows until you have completed 2 repeats of the chart, ending with Golden Gardens Chart row 16.

Body
Row 1 (RS): P to M, SM, work Golden Gardens Chart, SM, P to end.
Row 2 (WS): K to M, SM, work Golden Gardens Chart, SM, K to end.

Repeat the last two rows until you have completed 10 (10, 10, 10, 11, 11, 11, 12, 12, 12) total repeats of the chart, ending with row 16. Work Row 1 one more time, working Golden Gardens Chart row 1. Break yarn, leaving a long tail, and transfer all sts to scrap yarn. Set aside

Front
The front is worked flat from the hem up.

Split Hem
Loosely CO 78 (86, 96, 104, 112, 122, 130, 138, 148, 156) sts. K 5 rows.
Set-Up Row: K 58 (63, 68, 73, 78, 84, 90, 94, 101, 106), PM, K3, P2, K2, P2, K3, PM, K to end.
Row 1 (RS): K4, P to M, SM, work Golden Gardens Chart, SM, P to 4 before end, K4.
Row 2 (WS): K to M, SM, work Golden Gardens Chart, SM, K to end.

Repeat the last two rows until you have completed 1 repeat of the Golden Gardens Chart, ending with row 16.

Body
Row 1 (RS): P to M, SM, work Golden Gardens Chart, SM, P to end.
Row 2 (WS): K to M, SM, work Golden Gardens Chart, SM, K to end.

Repeat the last two rows until you have completed 8 (8, 8, 8, 9, 9, 9, 10, 10, 10) total repeats of the chart, ending with row 16.

Work Shoulders
Row 1 (RS): K 32 (35, 40, 43, 46, 50, 52, 56, 59, 62) (Left Shoulder), transfer 14 (16, 16, 18, 20, 22, 26, 26, 30, 32) sts to scrap yarn for Front Neck. **Optional:** Transfer remaining 32 (35, 40, 43, 46, 50, 52, 56, 59, 62) sts (Right Shoulder) to separate scrap yarn or a stitch holder. Alternatively, you can keep stitches on needle, unworked, until you have completed your Left Shoulder.
Row 2 (WS): Working only Left Shoulder sts, turn, BO 4 and work to end in pattern.
Row 3 and all odd-numbered rows: Work in pattern, no shaping.
Row 4: BO 2, work in pattern to end.
Row 6: Ssk, work in pattern to end.
Row 8: Ssk, work in pattern to end.

Continue in pattern with no more shaping until you have completed chart row 15. 24 (27, 32, 35, 38, 42, 44, 48, 51) sts. Break yarn leaving a long tail. Transfer all Left Shoulder sts to scrap yarn.

Join yarn and work Right Shoulder, beginning with a RS row.

Row 1 (RS): BO 4, P to end.
Row 2 and all even-numbered rows (WS): K.
Row 3: BO 2, P to end.
Row 5: P2tog, p to end.
Row 7: P2tog, p to end.

Continue in pattern, with no more shaping, until you have completed 15 rows. Break yarn leaving a long tail.
Using the tails, use the Kitchener stitch to attach the front and back shoulder sts, leaving 30 (32, 32, 34, 36, 38, 42, 42, 46, 48) sts still on scrap yarn for the Back Neck.

Sleeves (make 2)
The sleeve is worked flat from the cuff up.

Loosely cast on 32 (36, 42, 46, 50, 54, 60, 64, 68, 72) sts. K 5 rows.

Set-Up Row: K 10 (12, 15, 17, 19, 21, 24, 26, 28 30), PM, K3, P2, K2, P2, K3, PM, k to end.
Row 1 (RS): P to M, SM, work Golden Gardens Chart, SM, P to end.
Row 2 (WS): K to M, SM, work Golden Gardens Chart, SM, K to end.

Repeat last two rows 4 times (ending with a WS row), then work and Increase Row as follows:
Increase Row: P1, M1, P to M, SM, work Golden Gardens Chart, SM, P to 1 before end, M1, P1.

Continue in pattern, working an Increase Row every 8 (8, 8, 8, 8, 6, 6, 6, 6)th row until 48 (52, 58, 62, 66, 70, 76, 80, 84 88) sts remain.

Continue working sleeve in pattern with no more shaping until you have completed 5 (5, 5, 5, 5, 4, 4, 4, 4) total repeats of the Golden Gardens Chart, ending with row 16.

Work one more row in pattern.

BO loosely.

Sew sleeves to shoulders, centering the cable at the shoulder seam (Kitchener stitch seam), and distributing the sleeve evenly on either side before sewing in place.

Then, sew the sleeve/side seams, matching cuffs and underarm seams. Stop sewing the side seam just above the garter stitch border at the split hem.

Neckband

The neckband is picked up and worked in the round.

With RS facing, transfer 30 (32, 32, 34, 36, 38, 42, 42, 46, 48) sts from the Back Neck to the short circular needle. Knit across, decreasing 5 sts evenly across back of neck, PM. 25 (27, 27, 29, 31, 33, 37, 37, 41, 43). PU and K 12 sts along the left edge of the neck, PM. Transfer 14 (16, 16, 18, 20, 22, 26, 26, 30, 32) sts from the Front Neck to a spare needle, then K across, decreasing 3 sts evenly across the front of neck, PM. 11 (13, 13, 15, 17, 19, 23, 23, 27, 29) sts. PU and K 12 sts along the Right edge of the neck, place end of round marker. 60 (64, 64, 68, 72, 76, 84, 84, 92, 96) sts total.

Round 1: P.
Round 2: (K2tog, k to 2 before M, K2tog, sm, K to M, SM) twice.

Repeat Rounds 1 and 2 once more.

BO very loosely purlwise, or use a sewn bind off.

Finishing

Weave in ends and block lightly.

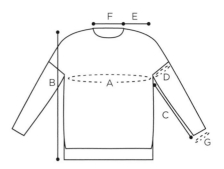

A 35.25 (38.75, 43.25, 46.75, 50.5, 55, 58.5, 62.25, 66.75, 70)"
B 29.75 (29.75, 29.75, 29.75, 32.5, 32.5, 32.5, 35.5, 35.5, 35.5)"
C 15.25 (15.25, 15.25, 15.25, 15.25, 15.25, 12.5, 12.5, 12.5, 12.5)"
D 10.75 (11.75, 13, 14, 14.75, 15.75, 17.25, 18, 19, 19.75)"
E 5.5 (6, 7.25, 7.75, 8.5, 9.5, 10, 10.75, 11.5, 12.25)"
F 6.75 (7.25, 7.25, 7.5, 8, 8.5, 9.5, 9.5, 10.25, 10.75)"
G 7.25 (8, 9.5, 10.25, 11.25, 12.25, 13.5, 14.5, 15.25, 16.25)"

Golden Gardens Chart

Chart grid numbered 12 11 10 9 8 7 6 5 4 3 2 1 across the top, rows 1–16 up the side.

Legend

purl
RS: purl stitch
WS: knit stitch

1/1 RC
sl1 to CN, hold in back. k1, k1 from CN

knit
RS: knit stitch
WS: purl stitch

1/1 RPC
sl1 to CN, hold in back. k1, p1 from CN

1/1 LPC
sl1 to CN, hold in front. p1. k1 from CN

1/1 LC
sl1 to CN, hold in front. k1, k1 from CN

CALM TIDE CARDIGAN

by Kristen TenDyke

FINISHED MEASUREMENTS

29 (33, 37, 41, 45, 49, 53, 57, 61, 65)"
finished bust measurement, buttoned;
garment is meant to be worn with 1–3" of
positive ease

YARN

Knit Picks Simply Cotton Worsted
(100% Organic Cotton; 164 yards/100g):
Marshmallow 24761, 4 (5, 5, 6, 6, 6, 7, 7, 8,
8) balls

NEEDLES

US 7 (4.5mm) 24" or longer circular
needles plus a set of 4 or 5 DPNs, or size
to obtain gauge

NOTIONS

Yarn Needle
Stitch Markers
Scrap Yarn or Stitch Holder
Seven 1" buttons

GAUGE

16 sts and 21 rows/rnds = 4" in St st in the
rnd and worked flat, blocked
16 sts and 24 rows = 4" in Garter Ridge
Pattern, blocked

Calm Tide Cardigan

Notes:

This sweater is knit from the top down. The neck and raglan are shaped from the top of the neck down to the underarm. At the underarm, the body and sleeve stitches are divided and some stitches are cast-on for the underarms of the body. The sleeve stitches are held while the body is knit down, with some waist shaping. The sleeve stitches are placed onto DPNs, stitches are picked up over the underarm cast-on stitches of the body, then the sleeve is knit down to the cuff. Stitches are picked up around the front neck shaping and yoke cast-on edges for the neckband, then the buttonband stitches are picked up and knit, and buttonholes worked on opposite side.

Garter Ridge Pattern (worked flat)
Row 1 (RS): Knit.
Row 2 (WS): Purl.
Rows 3-4: Knit.
Rep Rows 1–4 for pattern.

Garter Stitch (worked flat)
All Rows: Knit.

Stockinette Stitch (worked flat)
Row 1 (RS): Knit.
Row 2 (WS): Purl.
Rep Rows 1 and 2 for pattern.

Stockinette Stitch (worked in the rnd)
Rnd 1: Knit.
Rep Rnd 1 for pattern.

K2, P2 Ribbing (worked flat over a multiple of 4 sts)
Row 1 (WS): P3, *K2, P2; rep from * to last st, P1.
Row 2 (RS): K1, *K2, P2; rep from * to last 3 sts, K3.
Rep Rows 1 and 2 for pattern.

K2, P2 Ribbing (worked in the rnd over a multiple of 4 sts)
Rnd 1: *K1, P2, K1; rep from * around.
Rep Rnd 1 for pattern.

Cable Cast-on Method
Hold work so yarn is attached to sts on the left needle. K1, slip new st onto left needle; *insert right needle between first 2 sts on left needle and K1 from this position leaving the first st on the left needle, slip the new st from the right needle onto the left needle; rep from * for desired number of sts.

M1L: (make 1 left-slanting) Insert left needle tip from front to back, then knit.

M1LP: (make 1 left-slanting, P-wise) Insert left needle tip from back to front, then purl.

M1R: (make 1 right slanting) Insert left needle from back to front, then knit.

M1RP: (make 1 right-slanting, P-wise) Insert left needle tip from front to back, then purl tbl.

DIRECTIONS
Yoke
The yoke is worked flat from the neck down. A circular needle is recommended to accommodate the large number of sts.

Raglan
With circular needle, loosely CO 44 (46, 46, 48, 48, 50, 50, 52, 52, 54) sts.

Row 1 (WS): (place markers for raglan) P2 for front, PM, P8 for sleeve, PM, P24 (26, 26, 28, 28, 30, 30, 32, 32, 34) for back, PM, P8 for sleeve, PM, P2 for front.

Shape Raglan
Continue working in Garter Ridge Pattern, always keeping 1 st between the increases in St st while working the raglan shaping as follows. Be careful to only work the sections indicated for your size. It may be helpful to circle or highlight all the information for your size throughout the raglan shaping before beginning.

Body and Sleeve Inc Row (RS): *K to 1 st before next M, M1L, K1, SM, M1R, K to next M, M1L, SM, K1, M1R; rep from * 1 more time, K to end. 8 sts inc.
Work 1 WS row even in pattern.

Rep the last 2 rows 3 (2, 2, 2, 3, 3, 3, 3, 4, 4) more times. 76 (70, 70, 72, 80, 82, 82, 84, 92, 94) sts; 6 (5, 5, 5, 6, 6, 6, 6, 7, 7) sts each front, 16 (14, 14, 14, 16, 16, 16, 16, 18, 18) sts each sleeve and 32 (32, 32, 34, 36, 38, 38, 40, 42, 44) sts for back.

Sizes - (-, -, -, 45, 49, 53, 57, 61, 65)" only:
Shape Front Neck and Raglan
Neck, Body and Sleeve Inc Row (RS): K1, M1R, *K to 1 st before next M, M1L, K1, SM, M1R, K to next M, M1L, SM, K1, M1R; rep from * 1 more time, K to last st, M1L, K1. 10 sts inc.
Body Inc Row (WS): *Knit or purl in pattern to 1 st before next M, M1RP or M1R keeping in pattern, P1, SM, knit or purl in pattern to next M, SM, P1, M1LP or M1L keeping in pattern; rep from * once more, knit or purl to end in pattern. 4 sts inc.

Rep the last 2 rows - (-, -, -, 1, 2, 4, 5, 6, 7) more times. - (-, -, -, 108, 124, 152, 168, 190, 206) sts; - (-, -, -, 12, 15, 21, 24, 28, 31) sts each front, - (-, -, -, 20, 22, 26, 28, 32, 34) sts each sleeve and - (-, -, -, 44, 50, 58, 64, 70, 76) sts for back.

Sizes 29 (33, 37, 41, 45, 49, 53, 57, -, -)" only:
Neck, Body and Sleeve Inc Row (RS): K1, M1R, *K to 1 st before next M, M1L, K1, SM, M1R, K to next M, M1L, SM, K1, M1R; rep from * 1 more time, K to last st, M1L, K1. 10 sts increased.
Work 1 WS row even.

Rep the last 2 rows 2 (3, 3, 4, 2, 2, 0, 0, -, -) more times. 106 (110, 110, 122, 138, 154, 162, 178, -, -) sts; 12 (13, 13, 15, 18, 21, 23, 26, -, -) sts each front, 22 (22, 22, 24, 26, 28, 28, 30, -, -) sts each sleeve and 38 (40, 40, 44, 50, 56, 60, 66, -, -) sts for back.

All Sizes:
Next Row (RS): *K to 1 st before next M, M1L, K1, SM, M1R, K to next M, M1L, SM, K1, M1R; rep from * 1 more time, K to end. With RS still facing use the Cable Method to CO 3 sts. 11 sts inc.
Next Row (WS): Knit or purl in pattern to end, with WS still

facing, use the Cable Method to CO 3 sts. 3 sts inc; 120 (124, 124, 136, 152, 168, 176, 192, 204, 220) sts; 16 (17, 17, 19, 22, 25, 27, 30, 32, 35) sts each front, 24 (24, 24, 26, 28, 30, 30, 32, 34, 36) sts each sleeve and 40 (42, 42, 46, 52, 58, 62, 68, 72, 78) sts for back.

The front neck shaping is now complete. Continue working the raglan shaping in the Garter Ridge Pattern, maintaining 1 st in St st at each raglan marker, as follows:

Body and Sleeve Inc Row (RS): *K to 1 st before next M, M1L, K1, SM, M1R, K to next M, M1L, SM, K1, M1R; rep from * 1 more time, K to end. 8 sts inc.
Work 1 WS row even in pattern.

Rep the last 2 rows 0 (4, 9, 6, 6, 4, 5, 3, 2, 0) more times. 128 (164, 204, 192, 208, 208, 224, 224, 228, 228) sts; 17 (22, 27, 26, 29, 30, 33, 34, 35, 36) sts each front, 26 (34, 44, 40, 42, 40, 42, 40, 40, 38) sts each sleeve and 42 (52, 62, 60, 66, 68, 74, 76, 78, 80) sts for back.

Sizes 29 (33, -, -, -, -, -, -, -, -)" only:
Body and Sleeve Inc Row (RS): *K to 1 st before next M, M1L, K1, SM, M1R, K to next M, M1L, SM, K1, M1R; rep from * 1 more time, K to end. 8 sts inc.
Work 1 WS row even.

Sleeve Inc Row (RS): *K to next M, SM, M1R, K to next M, M1L, SM; rep from * 1 more time, K to end. 4 sts inc.
Work 1 WS row even.
Rep the last 4 rows 3 (1, -, -, -, -, -, -, -, -) more times. 176 (188, -, -, -, -, -, -, -, -) sts; 21 (24, -, -, -, -, -, -, -, -) sts each front, 42 (42, -, -, -, -, -, -, -, -) sts each sleeve and 50 (56, -, -, -, -, -, -, -, -) sts for back.

Sizes - (-, -, 41, 45, 49, 53, 57, 61, 65)" only:
Body and Sleeve Inc Row (RS): *K to 1 st before next M, M1L, K1, SM, M1R, K to next M, M1L, SM, K1, M1R; rep from * 1 more time, K to end. 8 sts inc.
Work 1 WS row even.

Body Inc Row (RS): *K to 1 st before next M, M1L, K1, SM, K to next M, SM, K1, M1R; rep from * 1 more time, K to end. 4 sts inc.
Work 1 WS row even.

Rep the last 4 rows - (-, -, 1, 1, 2, 2, 3, 4, 5) more times. - (-, -, 216, 232, 244, 260, 272, 288, 300) sts; - (-, -, 30, 33, 36, 39, 42, 45, 48) sts each front, - (-, -, 44, 46, 46, 48, 48, 50, 50) sts each sleeve and - (-, -, 68, 74, 80, 86, 92, 98, 104) sts for back.

All Sizes
Divide Body and Sleeves
Continue working all sts in St st.

Next Row (RS): K21 (24, 27, 30, 33, 36, 39, 42, 45, 48) front sts to first raglan M, remove M, place the next 42 (42, 44, 44, 46, 46, 48, 48, 50, 50) sts onto a st holder or scrap yarn for sleeve, remove raglan M, turn work so WS is facing and use the Cable Method to CO 4 (5, 6, 7, 8, 9, 10, 11, 12, 13) sts, PM for center of underarm then CO another 4 (5, 6, 7, 8, 9, 10, 11, 12, 13) sts, turn work so RS is facing, K50 (56, 62, 68, 74, 80, 86, 92, 98, 104) back sts to next M, remove M, place the next 42 (42, 44, 44, 46, 46, 48, 48, 50, 50) sts onto a st holder or waste yarn for sleeve, remove M, turn work so WS is facing and use the Cable Method to CO 4 (5, 6, 7, 8, 9,

10, 11, 12, 13) sts, PM for center of underarm then CO another 4 (5, 6, 7, 8, 9, 10, 11, 12, 13) sts, turn work so RS is facing, K21 (24, 27, 30, 33, 36, 39, 42, 45, 48) remaining front sts. 108 (124, 140, 156, 172, 188, 204, 220, 236, 252) sts remain.

Body
Shape Waist
Work 7 rows even in St st, ending after a WS row.

Dec Row (RS): *K to 4 sts before side M, K2tog, K2, SM, K2, SSK; rep from * once more, K to end. 4 sts dec.

Rep the last 8 rows 3 more times. 92 (108, 124, 140, 156, 172, 188, 204, 220, 236) sts remain.

Shape Hips
Work 9 rows even in St st, ending after a WS row.

Inc Row (RS): *K to 2 sts before side M, M1L, K2, SM, K2, M1R; rep from * once more, K to end. 4 sts dec.

Rep the last 10 rows 3 more times. 108 (124, 140, 156, 172, 188, 204, 220, 236, 252) sts.

Body should measure about 13.75" from underarm divide.

Garter Stitch Hem
Beginning with a WS row, knit 4 rows.

Begin K2, P2 Ribbing:
Row 1 (WS): P3, *K2, P2; rep from * to last st, P1.

Continue to work 6 more rows in K2, P2 Ribbing as established. BO all sts loosely in ribbing.

Sleeves (work both the same)
Place 42 (42, 44, 44, 46, 46, 48, 48, 50, 50) held sts from one sleeve onto 3 or 4 DPNs. Begin at center of underarm CO sts, PU and K 4 (5, 6, 7, 8, 9, 10, 11, 12, 13) sts, K to end of held sts then PU and K another 4 (5, 6, 7, 8, 9, 10, 11, 12, 13) sts along the remaining underarm CO sts. 50 (52, 56, 58, 62, 64, 68, 70, 74, 76) sts. PM for beginning of rnd and join to work in the rnd.

Shape Sleeve
Knit 7 (7, 5, 5, 4, 3, 3, 3, 2, 2) rnds.
Dec Rnd: K1, K2tog, K to last 3 sts, SSK, K1. 2 sts dec.

Rep the last 8 (8, 6, 6, 5, 4, 4, 4, 3, 3) rnds 1 (6, 6, 2, 4, 1, 1, 4, 3, 0) more times. 46 (38, 42, 52, 52, 60, 64, 60, 66, 74) sts remain.

[Knit 9 (9, 7, 7, 6, 5, 5, 5, 4, 4) rnds, then rep Dec Rnd] 5 (1, 3, 6, 6, 10, 10, 8, 11, 13) times. 36 (36, 36, 40, 40, 40, 44, 44, 44, 48) sts remain.

Piece should measure about 12.5 (12.5, 12.5, 12.5, 12.75, 13, 13, 13, 12.75, 13)" from underarm.

Hem
Work in Garter Stitch and K2, P2 Ribbing as follows:
Rnd 1: Purl.
Rnd 2: Knit.

Rep Rnds 1–2 once more, then work 7 rnds in K2, P2 Ribbing. BO all sts loosely in ribbing.

Finishing
Weave in ends, wash and block to diagram.

Neckband

With RS facing, begin at right front neck edge, PU and K 3 sts along front neck BO sts, 12 (13, 13, 14, 16, 17, 17, 18, 20, 21) sts evenly along right front neck to yoke CO sts, 42 (44, 44, 46, 46, 48, 48, 50, 50, 52) sts along CO sts (1 st for each CO st, excluding 1 selvedge st at each edge), 12 (13, 13, 14, 16, 17, 17, 18, 20, 21) sts evenly along left front neck to BO sts, then 3 sts along front neck BO sts. 72 (76, 76, 80, 84, 88, 88, 92, 96, 100) sts.

Work flat in Garter Stitch for 4 rows.

Begin K2, P2 Ribbing:
Row 1 (WS): P3, *K2, P2; rep from * to last st, P1.

Continue to work 6 more rows in K2, P2 Ribbing as established. BO all sts loosely in ribbing.

Buttonband

With RS of left front facing, begin at top edge of neckband, PU and K 92 sts (for all sizes) evenly along neckband and left front edge.

Work flat in Garter Stitch for 4 rows.

Begin K2, P2 Ribbing:
Row 1 (WS): P3, *K2, P2; rep from * to last st, P1.
Continue to work 6 more rows in K2, P2 Ribbing as established. BO all sts loosely in ribbing.

Buttonhole Band

With RS of right front facing, begin at lower edge of right front, PU and K 92 sts (for all sizes) evenly along right front and neckband edge.

Work flat in Garter Stitch for 4 rows.

Begin K2, P2 Ribbing:
Row 1 (WS): P3, *K2, P2; rep from * to last st, P1.
Work 2 more rows in K2, P2 Ribbing as established.
Buttonhole Row (RS): K3, YO, P2tog, *(K2, P2) 3 times, YO, K2tog, (P2, K2) 3 times, YO, P2tog; rep from * 2 more times, K3.

Work 3 more rows in K2, P2 Ribbing as established. BO all sts loosely in ribbing.

Sew buttons opposite buttonholes.
Weave in ends. Block again if desired.

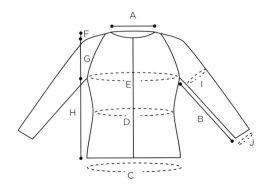

A 6 (6.5, 6.5, 7, 7, 7.5, 7.5, 8, 8, 8.5)"
B 14.5 (14.5, 14.5, 14.5, 14.75, 15, 15, 15, 14.75, 15)"
C 29 (33, 37, 41, 45, 49, 53, 57, 61, 65)"
D 25 (29, 33, 37, 41, 45, 49, 53, 57, 61)"
E 29 (33, 37, 41, 45, 49, 53, 57, 61, 65)"
F 1"
G 6 (6, 6.25, 7, 7.25, 7.75, 8, 8.25, 9, 9.25)"
H 15.75"
I 12.5 (13, 14, 14.5, 15.5, 16, 17, 17.5, 18.5, 19)"
J 9 (9, 9, 10, 10, 10, 11, 11, 11, 12)"

Abbreviations							
BO	bind off	M	marker		stitch	TBL	through back loop
cn	cable needle	M1	make one stitch	RH	right hand	TFL	through front loop
CC	contrast color	M1L	make one left-leaning	rnd(s)	round(s)	tog	together
CDD	Centered double dec		stitch	RS	right side	W&T	wrap & turn (see
CO	cast on	M1R	make one right-lean-	Sk	skip		specific instructions
cont	continue		ing stitch	Sk2p	sl 1, k2tog, pass		in pattern)
dec	decrease(es)	MC	main color		slipped stitch over	WE	work even
DPN(s)	double pointed	P	purl		k2tog: 2 sts dec	WS	wrong side
	needle(s)	P2tog	purl 2 sts together	SKP	sl, k, psso: 1 st dec	WYIB	with yarn in back
EOR	every other row	PM	place marker	SL	slip	WYIF	with yarn in front
inc	increase	PFB	purl into the front and	SM	slip marker	YO	yarn over
K	knit		back of stitch	SSK	sl, sl, k these 2 sts tog		
K2tog	knit two sts together	PSSO	pass slipped stitch	SSP	sl, sl, p these 2 sts tog		
KFB	knit into the front and		over		tbl		
	back of stitch	PU	pick up	SSSK	sl, sl, sl, k these 3 sts		
K-wise	knitwise	P-wise	purlwise		tog		
LH	left hand	rep	repeat	St st	stockinette stitch		
		Rev St st	reverse stockinette	sts	stitch(es)		

Knit Picks yarn is both luxe and affordable—a seeming contradiction trounced! But it's not just about the pretty colors; we also care deeply about fiber quality and fair labor practices, leaving you with a gorgeously reliable product you'll turn to time and time again.

THIS COLLECTION FEATURES

Stroll
Fingering Weight
75% Superwash Merino Wool,
25% Nylon

Comfy
Fingering Weight
75% Pima Cotton, 25% Acrylic

Shine Sport
Sport Weight
60% Pima Cotton, 40% Modal®

CotLin
DK Weight
70% Tanguis Cotton, 30% Linen

Simply Cotton
Worsted Weight
100% Organic Cotton

Swish DK
DK Weight
100% Superwash Merino Wool

Comfy Worsted
Worsted Weight
75% Pima Cotton, 25% Acrylic

View these beautiful yarns and
more at www.KnitPicks.com